Going Fishing

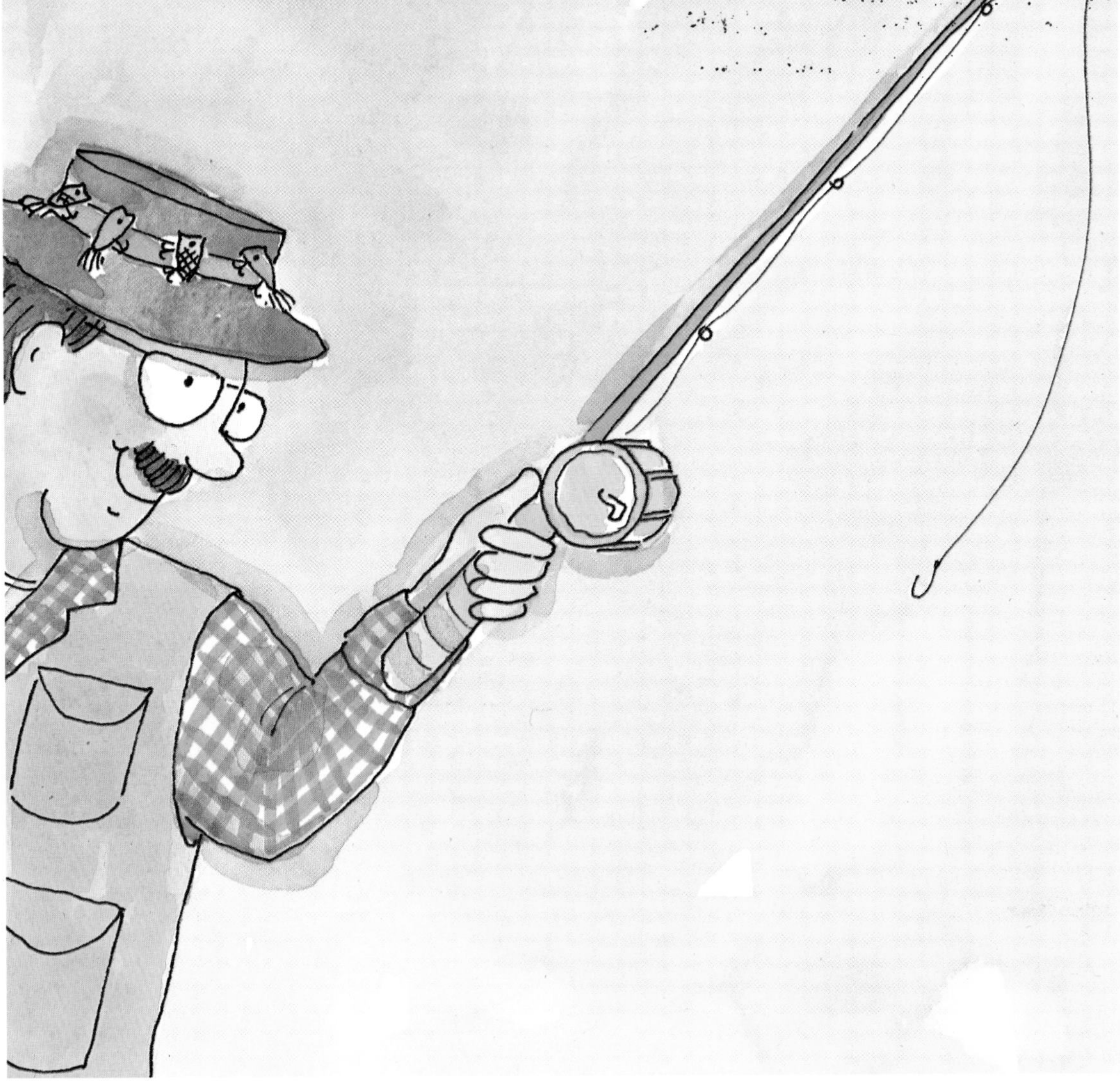

Written by Polly Peterson
Illustrated by Shelley Dieterichs

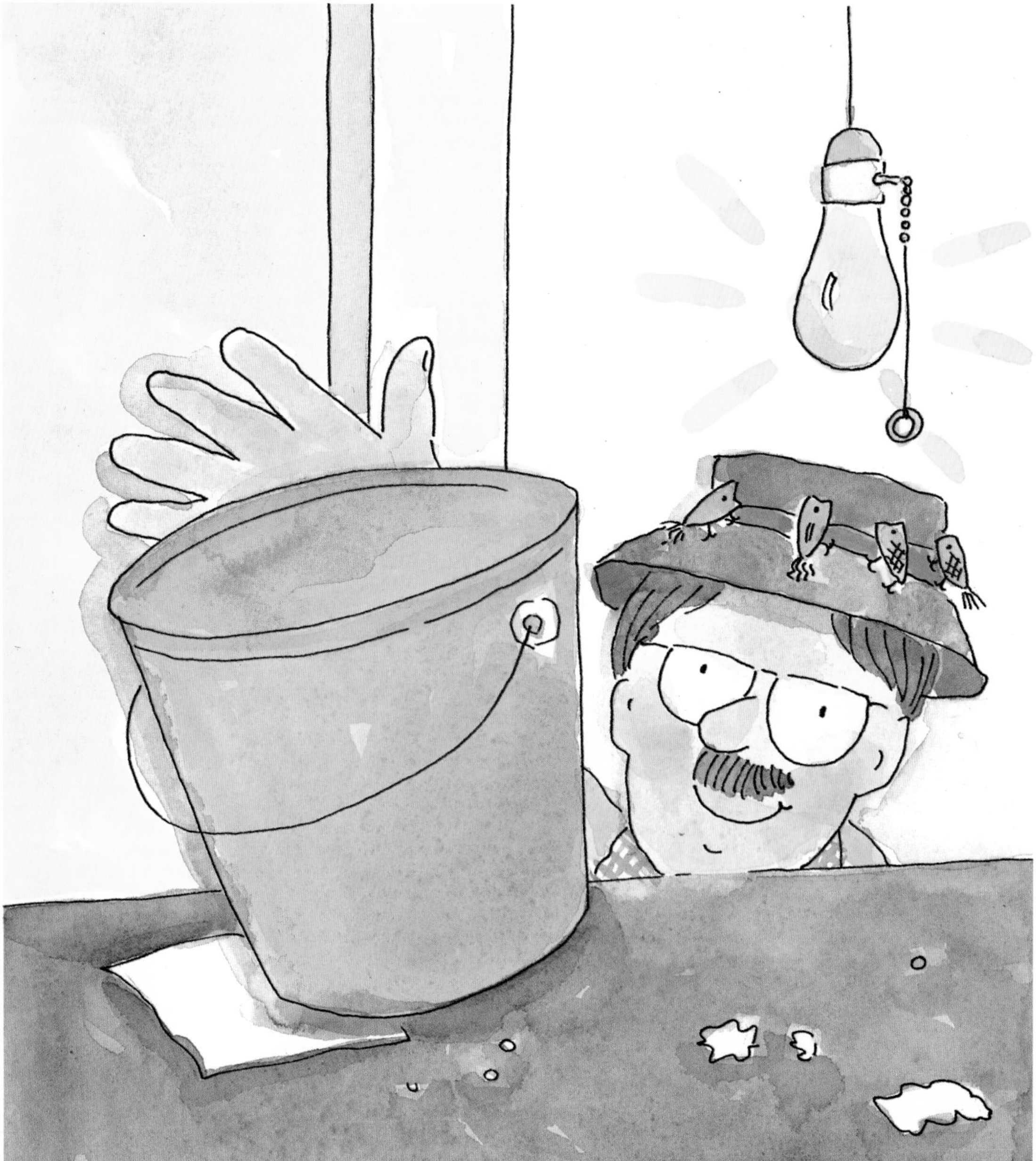

I take my pail,

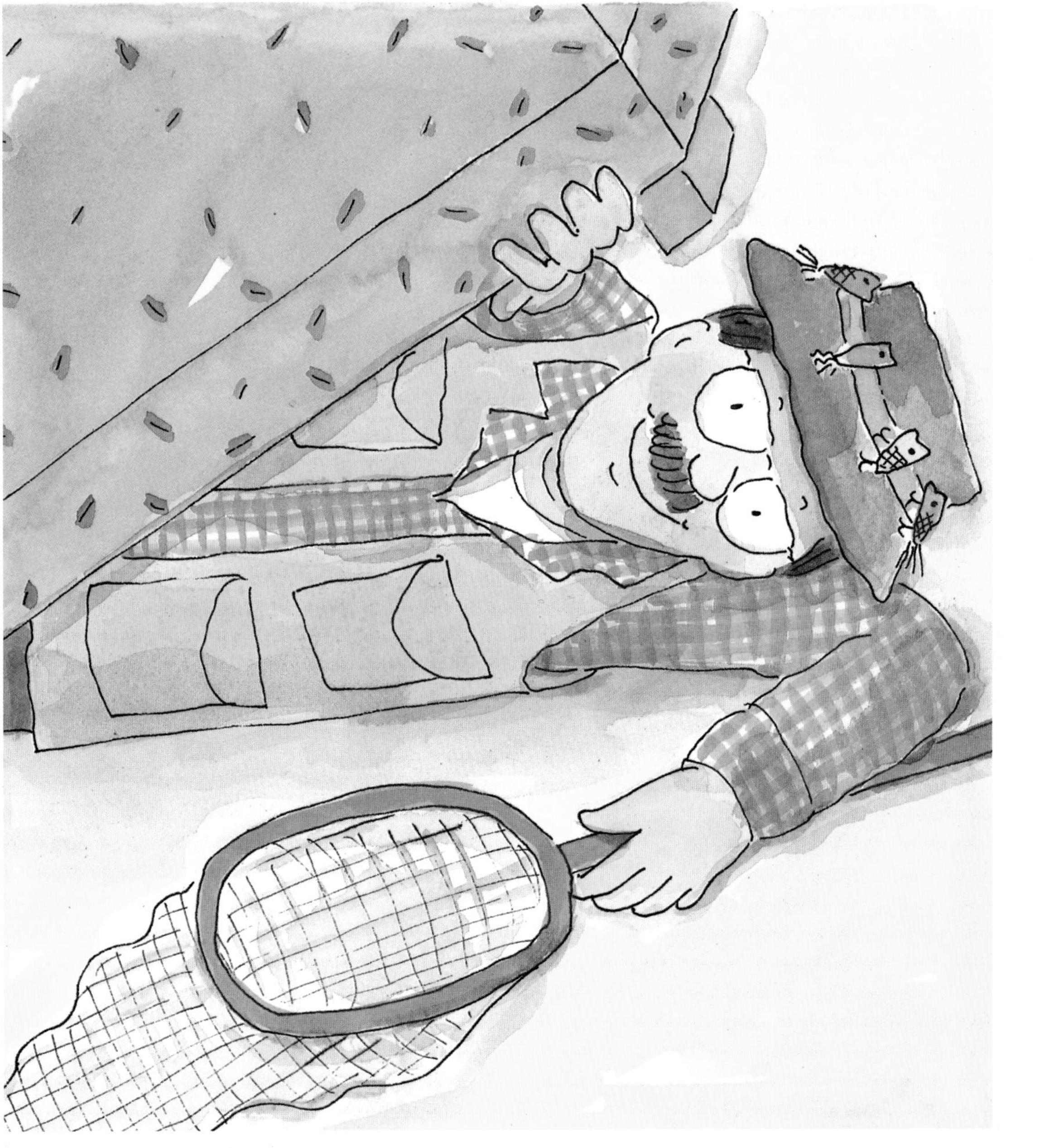

and my net,

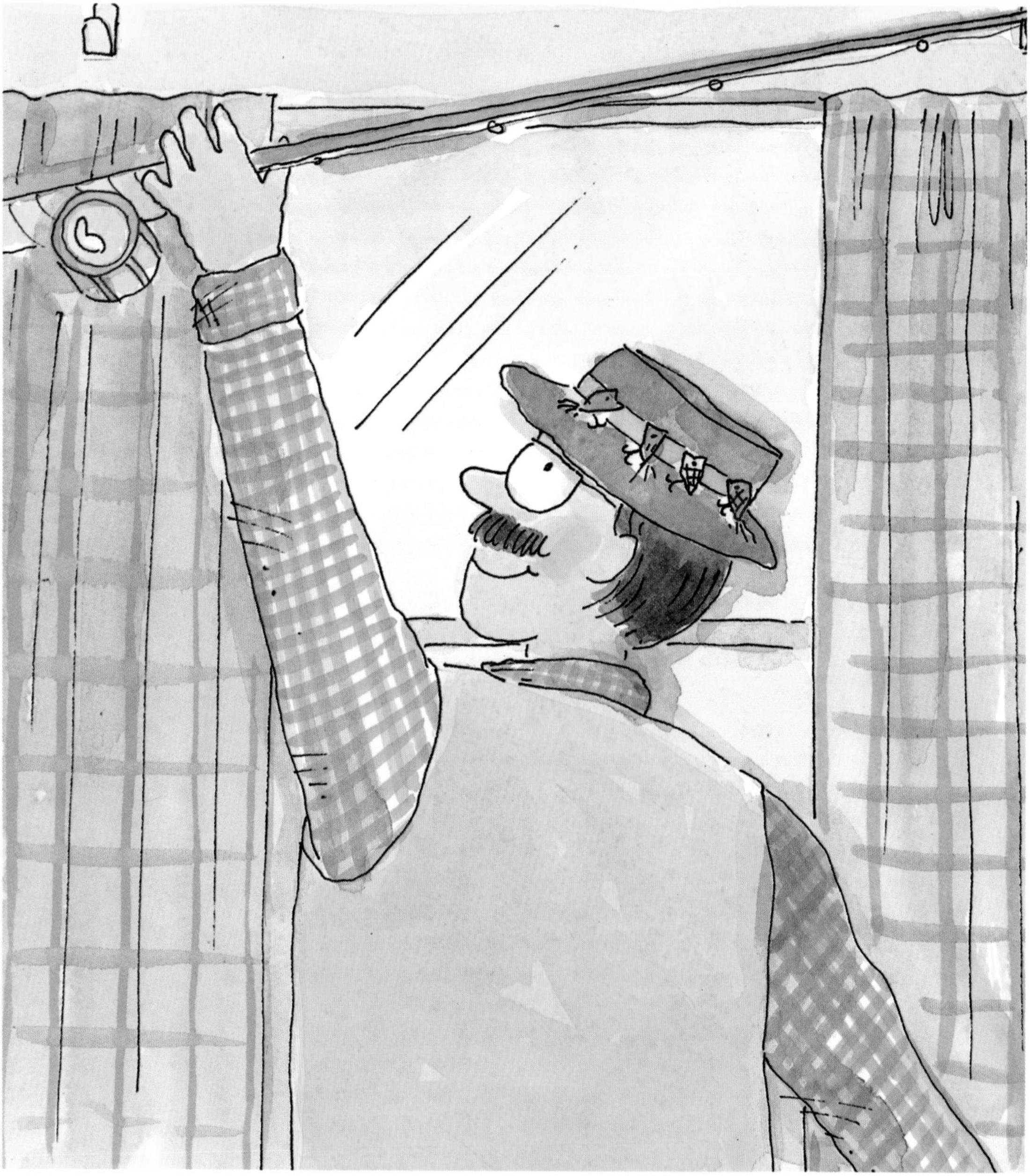

and my pole,

y pet,

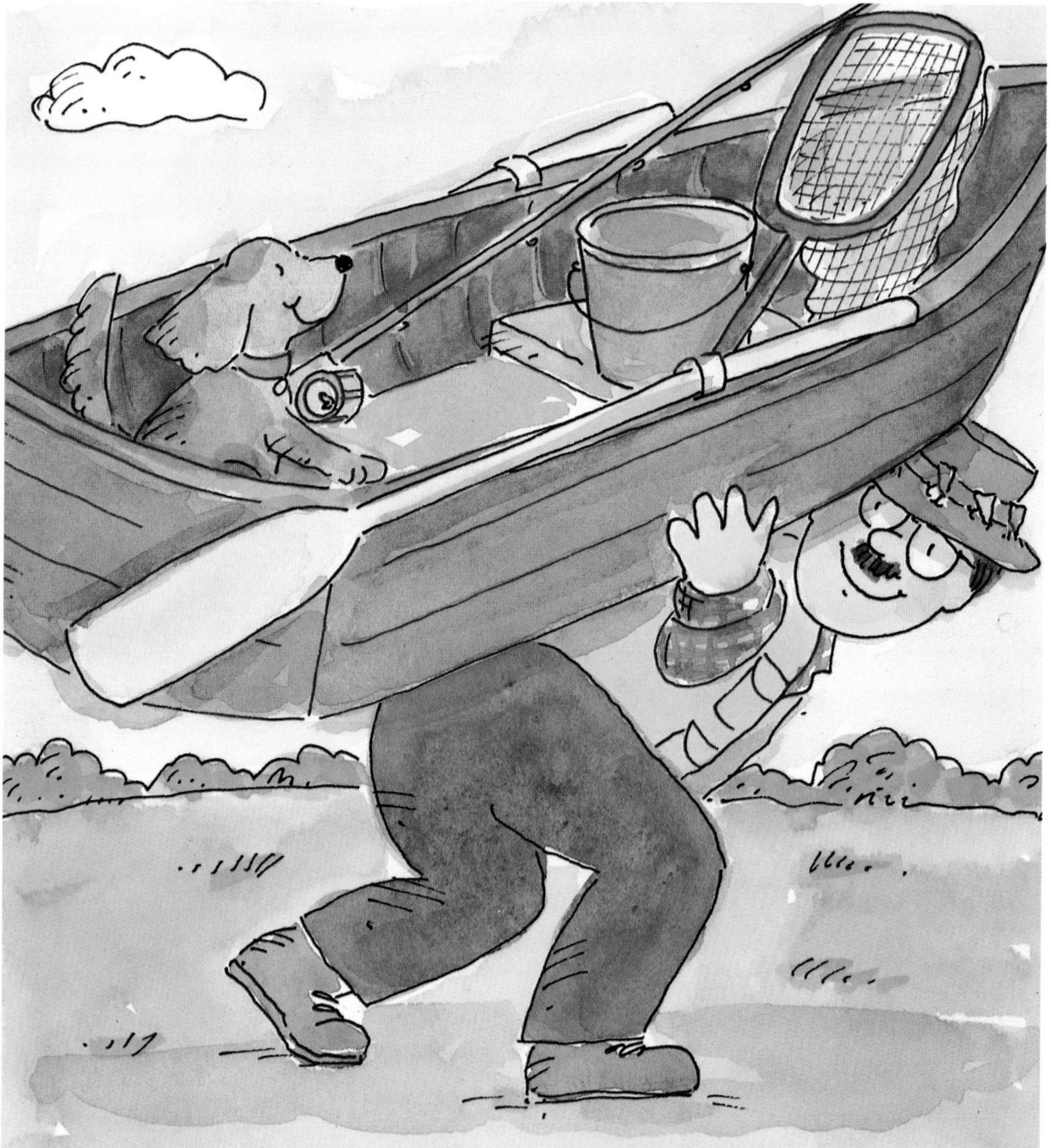

and my boat,

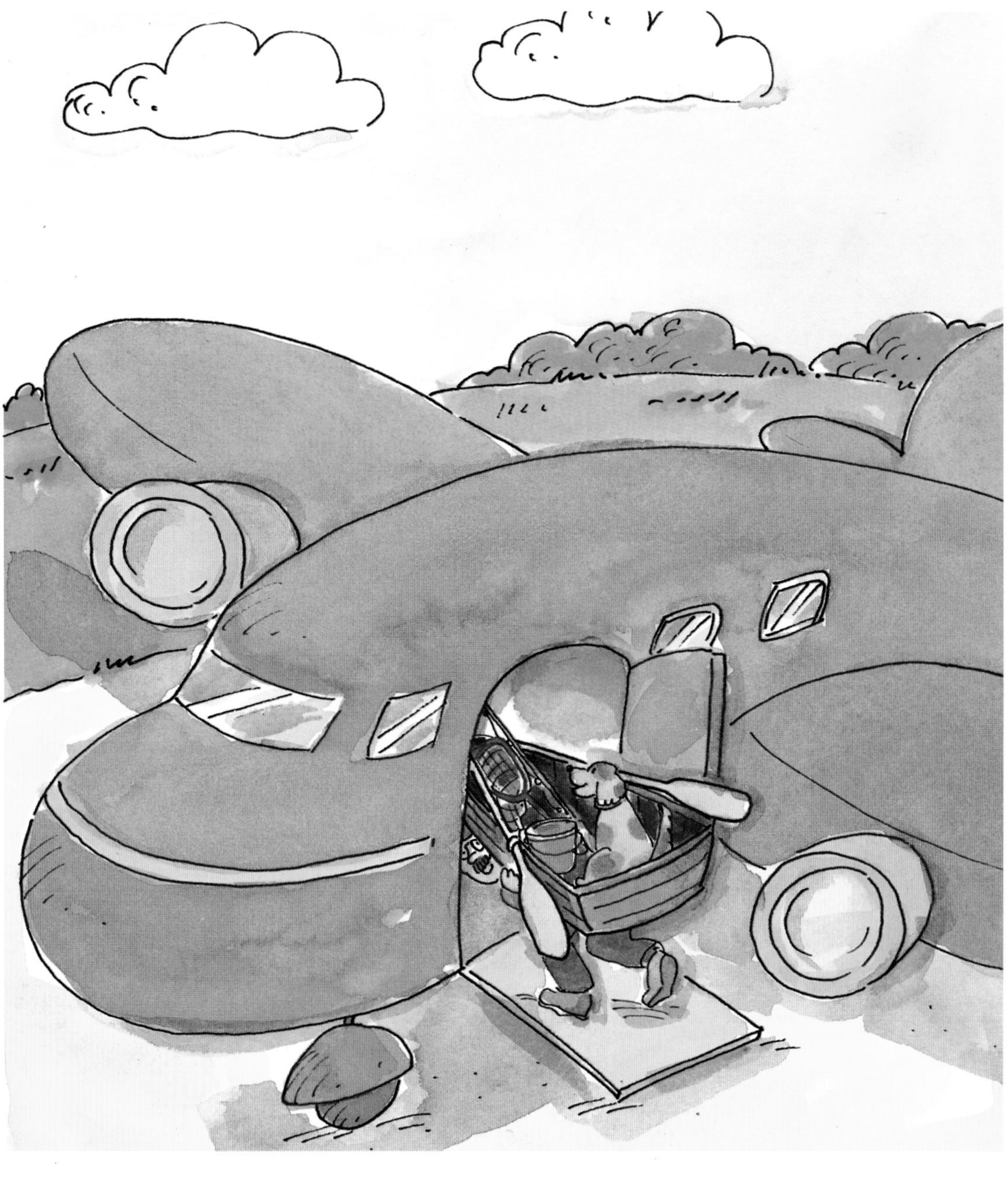

and my jet,

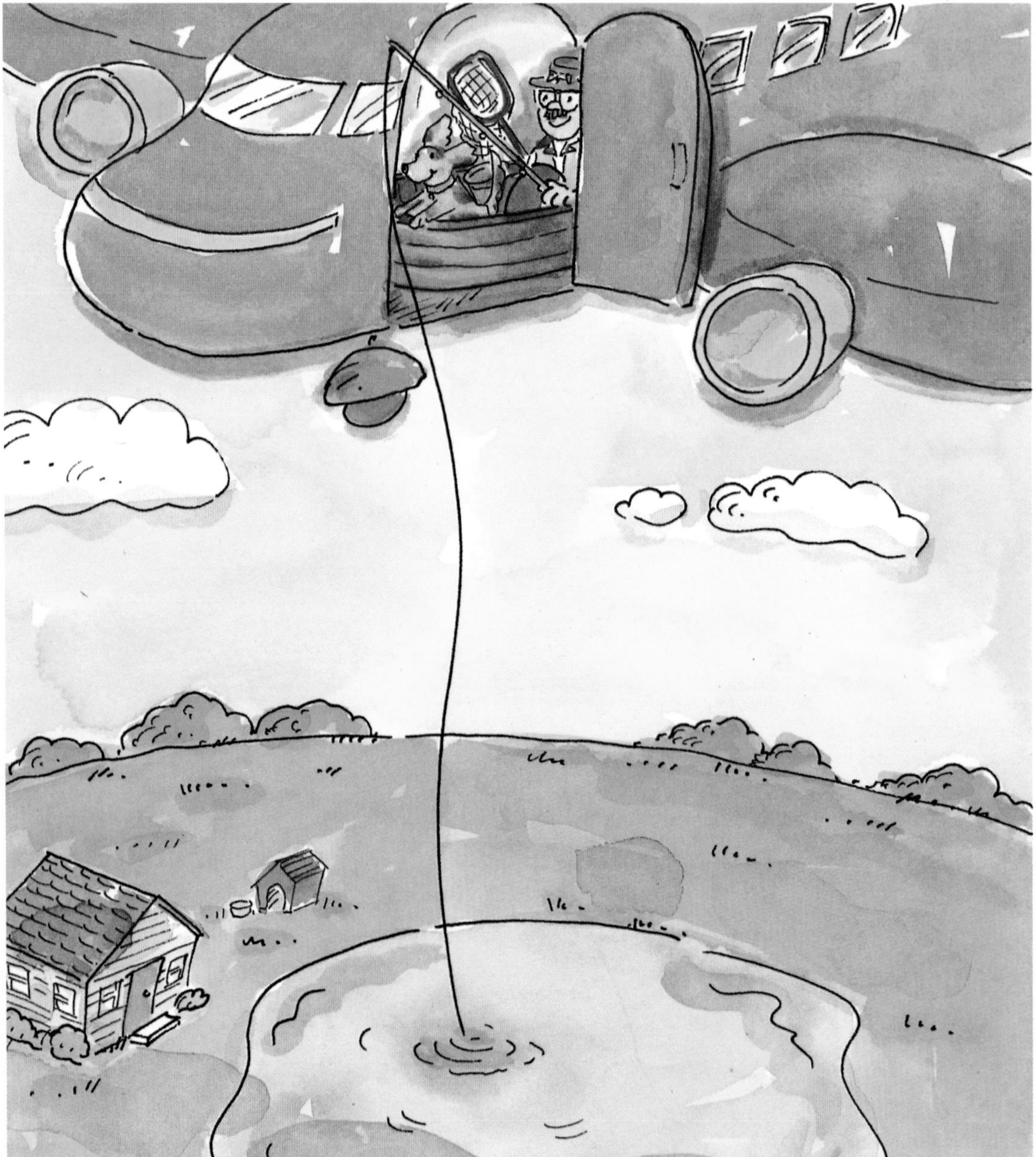

and go fishing.